Uncommon Grounds

Ash Wednesday Reflections from a Coffee Shop

Uncommon Grounds

Ash Wednesday Reflections from a Coffee Shop

Michael Tutterow

Uncommon Grounds: Ash Wednesday Reflections from a Coffee Shop
ISBN: Softcover 979-8-89532-002-0
Copyright © 2024 by Michael Tutterow

Parson's Porch Books is an imprint of Parson's Porch & Company (PP&C) in Cleveland, Tennessee. PP&C is a self-funded charity which earns money by publishing books of noted authors, representing all genres. Its face and voice is **David Russell Tullock** (dtullock@parsonsporch.com).

Parson's Porch & Company *turns books into bread & milk* by sharing its profits with the poor.

www.parsonsporch.com

Contents

More than coffee

For more than a year an ecumenical group of clergy had been meeting on Thursday mornings to share coffee together. Most of us had come to the community within the past two years. So the weekly meetings had no agenda other than for us to get to know one another.

One January one of the members of the group suggested we try something new together for Ash Wednesday – *"Ashes to Go,"* he called it. In some larger urban areas, clergy had begun the season of Lent by taking to the streets and sharing ashes with those "on the go." It turned into more than catching busy parishioners who might be unable to attend sanctuary services. They found even those who might never wish to darken the door of a church were surprisingly open and interested in engaging in the ancient ritual.

Several in the group liked the idea. So we divided the day into "shifts" and we signed up for the times that would work for us. Come that first Ash Wednesday, I arrived for what became the first of many of the most memorable experiences in my 35 years as a pastor.

Ten years later, the experiences of sharing ashes in a coffee shop have marked me as clearly as ashes traced on a forehead. Short but deeply personal conversations took place on those days. People opened up to me in ways that did not always happen at church. Some were my own church members; others were strangers who stopped by out of curiosity, or those who found some long dormant desire reawakened by a black cross smudged on my forehead.

In that common, everyday place, something uncommon was happening. More and more I began to realize that my colleagues and I weren't taking something holy "out there" to people. Something sacred was already happening "out there" and we were fortunate to see it and experience it.

This book was fresh-brewed in a local coffee shop. Each Ash Wednesday the conversations and observations percolated throughout the day as I wrote in a journal. And by late afternoon, I was able to pour them into a common cup to be shared during Ash Wednesday worship with my church family.

My hope is that these words invite you to take a seat alongside me and eavesdrop on these coffee conversations. Savor them, like a good cup of coffee brewed from the common grounds of human hope and longing. And may it help you sense that each of us are part of something uncommon happening all around us.

Michael Tutterow, April 2024

"Grounded"

"Beware of practicing your piety before others in order to be seen by them; for then you have no reward from your Father in heaven. 2So whenever you give alms, do not sound a trumpet before you, as the hypocrites do in the synagogues and in the streets, so that they may be praised by others. Truly I tell you, they have received their reward. 3But when you give alms, do not let your left hand know what your right hand is doing, 4so that your alms may be done in secret; and your Father who sees in secret will reward you.

5 "And whenever you pray, do not be like the hypocrites; for they love to stand and pray in the synagogues and at the street corners, so that they may be seen by others. Truly I tell you, they have received their reward. 6But whenever you pray, go into your room and shut the door and pray to your Father who is in secret; and your Father who sees in secret will reward you..

16 "And whenever you fast, do not look dismal, like the hypocrites, for they disfigure their faces so as to show others that they are fasting. Truly I tell you, they have received their reward. 17But when you fast, put oil on your head and wash your face, 18so that your fasting may be seen not by others but by your Father who is in secret; and your Father who sees in secret will reward you"

Matthew 6:1-6, 16-18, *New Revised Standard Version.*

––––––––––

A theme for tonight's Ash Wednesday reflection eluded me until this morning. As I sat in my home office and reflected on some meaning for our journey through this Lenten season, the word "grounded" came to mind.

Planes get "grounded,"
    brought down to earth for good reason
        a weather delay,
            a safety issue,
                something that makes it dangerous to fly up high.
    People can fly too high, too.
        But people who are grounded
            are those folk we know
                who are down to earth,
                    who are centered, solid, rooted and real.

    Lent is the season where we are called back to the
            ground of our being,
        brought back down from our lofty attitudes and
                invited to go low,
            to be humble – from the Latin word "*humus*,"
                meaning "soil" or "ground."

To be humble is to be grounded. So I chose *"Grounded"*
as the title for this reflection to kick off the season of
Lent.

Then I headed to *Starbucks* where I took a shift in
sharing the symbols of Ash Wednesday with anyone
who came by the coffee shop and desired it. And I
hoped the rest of the reflection would come to me
there.

It did.

For while there at *Starbucks*
    the name "grounded" took on new meaning
        as I smelled the aroma of fresh "ground" coffee!

That's when it occurred to me that *Starbucks*
    was precisely the place to begin the Lenten journey,

for the coffee shop became for me a parable
    about this season.

Flavor and aroma were only possible if the coffee was
    first "ground."
  Only when the hard-shell of the coffee bean is broken
    and the bean itself "ground" up
  can the water then wash over the grounds
    and release the fragrance and flavor hidden within.

So in a coffee shop,
  with ashes
    (aren't these also "grounds" of another kind?)
  smeared across my forehead,
    came the Lenten invitation
        to break open the hardness of my heart,
          to bring my pride back down to earth,
            and to allow the grace of God to wash over me
      and release the flavor and aroma of being
            human in a way that others might enjoy.

A clergy colleague marked me with ashes and words of
grace. She then entrusted to me the same task for the
next hour. I nestled into a chair, sipped some coffee,
and in between guests seeking to be grounded
themselves, jotted down the notes that make up this
reflection.

Sharing the ashes with others today grounded me in
some truths.

First, our mortality.
Ashes...to ashes, dust to dust.

It is our shared reality and shared destiny.

Life is finite and will one day come to an end
      for each of us,
            for all of us.
A hard truth. A sobering truth (though not necessarily a
      somber one).

Those who came to me this morning were of all ages;
      young, old, middle aged.
            Strangers, friends, even family.

And we are all mortal.
   We are human humus.
      Dust of the earth, to which we shall one day return.

It brought to mind an Ash Wednesday service several
            years ago.
   We had gathered in the sanctuary for prayer and
            reflection
            and then each of us walked away with the ashen
            mark of the cross on our foreheads.

As I walked back to my office,
   others walked to the preschool wing to pick up their
            children.
            That's where some women who had been in an
            ESL class upstairs saw them.

I heard the first one tap on the door frame of my office,
   and in broken English and hand gestures
      she asked for me to sign her forehead too.

I did.

And then from behind her stepped a shy, lovely-faced
        preschool child
    with the promise of her whole life still ahead of her.
        Yet her mother gestured
            that I should mark her for death, too.
I knelt down to do so,
    eye to eye with her child,
        with those young eyes staring at me,
    and in that moment felt myself grounded,
        reminded of the brevity of life,
            the fragility of life,
    and thus the preciousness of life.

For the next few minutes,
    a steady stream of Latina women and children filed
        into my office,
    all of us reminded about death
        so we would all cherish more closely life.

With strangers and loved ones today, this truth again
        grounds me:
    that as brief as life may be, it still can be full;
that if we will choose life –
    if we will choose to do the things that lead to life –
        then death need not frighten us.

That if we choose life,
    and the things that lead to life,
        then death will never be the last word for us.

Another truth grounded me today.

Our brokenness also unites us.
The first person who came to me at *Starbucks* was a
young woman I did not know.

A stranger, and yet she was a sister.
    For she bore the same mark on her forehead;
        She, too, walked away smudged for all to see.

And I marked her.
    My dirty fingers left that smudge on her.

And later left it on those I did know.
And left it on those in my own family who know me,
    and who know what that smudge on my forehead represents,
        the brokenness that I pretend cannot be seen
            but they know it,
                they have seen it visible in ways as clear as
                    the mark on my forehead tonight.

We – you and me – share this brokenness.
    On this day, we carry the mark for all to see:
        the mark left on us by others,
            the mark we have left on others,
                the mark that reminds us of those times
    we have tried to rise above the lower elements of our life
        only to sink deeper in the dirt.

And yet.

And yet in our brokenness, a greater truth grounds us still.
    We are dust – but *sacred* dust.

For we also share a Maker, One who fashioned us from the dust
    and One who became dust Himself.
        We share a Maker who loved us in our mortality,
            Who chose to become One of us in our humanity.

And this One reminds us there is something sacred about us,
    something miraculous even about our dust.

For hidden in our hemoglobin is iron,
   tiny particles of distant stars that long ago
      were sown in the dust from which we were made.

When I went to mark each person today,
   I became aware that each face I touched was unique;
      I knelt and stared into eyes deep with color and beauty.

All those who came were more than dust. Something
   from the stars in all of them.

Which is why the ashes of this day mark us with the cross,
   reminding us one more time when we stare in the
      mirror to wash our faces tonight
   that it is the cross that lifts us out of the dust.

The cross – the instrument of death –
   turns out to be a sign of life
      a sign that grace is greater than guilt,
      that hope is more powerful than despair,
         that love is stronger than death.

Our mortality, our brokenness and God's grace – these
unite us.

And from the coffee shop, one more common ground.

Our longing reveals a shared hope.
   The hope that we would live as more than dust;
      the hope that from the fertile ground of faith we
         might rise beyond the dust;
            the hope that, with Jesus, we mortals might
            become more fully human.

A couple came to Starbucks for coffee. He glanced at
me as they entered. Then he looked again – staring for a

moment at the mark on my forehead. She ventured a look out the corner of her eye as she went to the restroom.

Like any customers, they stood at the counter and waited for their coffees. But their continued glances told me they wanted more.

"Are you a priest?" he asked me.

"No, but I am a pastor."

"Would you bless us? My girlfriend, she is from Columbia ...Would you...?"

His voice trailed off as he stared at me.

In his voice was hope. The ashes may have been part of her religious tradition, but he was hoping now it could be something they could share.

Hope that I would accept him.

Hope that the God I represented would accept him, too, I suppose.

Hope that whatever I was doing there I might include them, too.

What will happen, we all wonder, when we turn to others, when we recognize we are dust but want to be more?

This is the hope we all have –
    to love and to be loved;
    to share ourselves with another;
        to find a connection that makes us feel like we are
            more than dust;
    to hear a word that allows us to become more than dust.

So they sat down and I knelt between them –
    grounded myself between them –
        And spoke words of truth:
    that we are dust, mortal, finite;
        that we are forgiven, loved, redeemed.

And then marked them –
    Marked them with the cross,
        with the sign of death that leads to life;
            with the sign that God sees more in us than
            we sometimes see in ourselves;
                with the sign of love and acceptance
                that gives birth to hope.

We all three then stood. He thanked me.
    And then, reaching for his wallet, wondered if he
        could give a gift.

"No thank you," I replied. "This is a gift for you."

As they left, he held the door for her.
    Grace making him gracious.
Reminding me anew how God's love makes us more
        than dust after all.

This is the Ash Wednesday Gospel according to
Starbucks. Thanks be to God. Amen.

———

This Ash Wednesday reflection was written from notes made at Starbucks on February 13, 2013.

"Pray Like This..."

"When you are praying, do not heap up empty phrases as the Gentiles do; for they think that they will be heard because of their many words. 8Do not be like them, for your Father knows what you need before you ask him. 9Pray then in this way:

Our Father in heaven, hallowed be your name. 10Your kingdom come. Your will be done, on earth as it is in heaven. 11Give us this day our daily bread. 12And forgive us our debts, as we also have forgiven our debtors. 13And do not bring us to the time of trial, but rescue us from the evil one. For the kingdom and the power and the glory are yours forever. Amen."

Matthew 6:5-13, *New Revised Standard Version*

"With a God like this loving you, you can pray very simply. Like this:

'Our Father in heaven, Reveal who you are. 10Set the world right; Do what's best — as above, so below. 11Keep us alive with three square meals. 12Keep us forgiven with you and forgiving others. 13Keep us safe from ourselves and the Devil.

You're in charge! You can do anything you want! You're ablaze in beauty! Yes. Yes. Yes.'"

Matthew 6:9-13, *The Message*

"Pray like this..."

This holy season begins with an invitation to pray, to use the words of Jesus and allow them to shape the way we speak to God, the way we think about our world and our loved ones and our friends and even our enemies. Jesus offers us these words, not as a substitute for our own words (though the words themselves can be helpful to pray), but as a way of shaping our prayers so they are personal, so they are passionate; prayers that are real and honest and hopeful.

So I've been thinking this week what it means to "pray like this." And I had some thoughts put together to share, and then I went to *Starbucks* this morning to share with my colleagues in the "ashes to go" ministry and I came away with some different thoughts. Like last year, my reflection for tonight will be shaped by my journal notes of what happened this morning. Of all places, *Starbucks* gave me new insights to what Jesus might mean when He said, "Pray like this...".

"Our Father..."

I arrived this morning at 8:30 to find Ted Smith from First Presbyterian Church quietly reading at a table, the ashes in a small container in front of him. He and I chatted for a few minutes, and then I asked him to mark me with the ashes as the final act of his "shift."

As he walked away, it struck me anew that I am connected to a wider Body of Christ, and that each time I pray the prayer Jesus taught, I share words that echo around the world in every language and every culture. But also a larger church here in Cartersville. For each time I pray to "our Father," I am praying not just to

20

"my" Father, but also to Ted's Father and to Doug's Father, to Mary's Father and Eric's Father and Julie's Father. We all represent various religious traditions, but we all find our common ground on earth in our Father in heaven.

And when we all find a way to work together, to bear witness to our one Father, it seems to me that we are, in fact, hallowing God's name. That we are causing the name of God to become greater and more important to us whenever we refuse to allow petty things to divide us in a way that lowers God's name and lowers the view others have of God's name.

When I pray these opening words and when I live this hallowed way with my brothers and sisters; when I actually *see* them as my brothers and sisters, it helps me to see that the Kingdom of God I pray will one day come is, in many ways, already taking shape, that it is already coming and waiting only on me to welcome it and receive it.

"Thy will be done on earth as it is in heaven..."

When Ted marked me with the ashes, it felt like a commissioning. We were playing tag team – he was now entrusting to me the ashes and the words of blessing that had been given to him earlier that morning by Mary, and which would be given to Doug in the next hour after me. In receiving the ashes and his words, I was accepting his charge – I was agreeing to do what he had been doing.

So is it not possible to hear this line of Jesus' prayer also as a commissioning? That when Jesus gives us these words, is He not handing off to me and to you the task of not just praying for God to send something, but praying that we would take what has already been given and embody and continue His work? He gives us these words – *His words to the world* – so that we can share them with others. He gives us these hopes – *His hopes for the world* – in hopes that you and I will make them our own and freely offer them to others. Isn't praying for the Kingdom to come really a prayer that what Jesus most desires would become the very thing we would most desire as well?

"Give us this day our daily bread."

It is, frankly, the phrase I am most familiar with, the phrase I most repeat though I change one word more often than I realize. "Our" bread too often, I fear, is mostly "my" bread. My prayers are lists of needs for today and tomorrow for myself and for others I know who are in my circle of concern, which tends to be a somewhat smaller circle than God's Kingdom.

Which made me wonder at how little time I spend on the first phrases. Truth be told, I must confess my needs and wishes receive far more of my passion than "God's Kingdom" or "God's will" does in my life. How about you? What would it mean for us to linger longer on those first phrases, to pray with greater awareness of the Fatherhood of God, greater understanding of the will of God, greater desire to be a part of welcoming the Kingdom into our lives?

So, there in *Starbucks*, I was pushed to ask how a deeper understanding of these first phrases might help me to see that the bread I do pray for really is "our" bread, too. And if it's "our" bread, then that means my prayer to be fed must also become a prayer that Ted and Mary, Julie and Eric and Doug and Charlie, and Nena and Kevin and Julie and Mark and Jessica and a whole host of others will also be fed today, will be fed each day. And maybe the only way that can happen is if I learn to want a little less bread for myself and more bread for them. Which leads well into the next phrase: "Forgive us our trespasses..."

"And forgive us our trespasses, as we forgive those who trespass against us."

When Doug Belisle came to relieve me at the end of my shift, he wanted to know how I had been marking the people who came to me and what I had been saying to them. You see, this was Doug's first time to do Ash Wednesday – *ever*. So he had been reading to prepare for it, but since he had actually never received the ashes before let alone given them, he was still not quite sure what to do or what to say.

The irony of one Baptist telling another Baptist how to do Ash Wednesday is not lost on me since we stand in the shallow end of the liturgical pool! The proverb about "the blind leading the blind" comes to mind, as does the request to forgive us "for we know not what we do."

Nevertheless, I shared with him what I had been doing and saying. In the more intimate, one-on-one setting of *Starbucks*, there is time to be with those who come for the ashes, to talk together and offer a few more words with the ashes that will mark them the rest of the day. I explained to Doug how the ashes remind us that, indeed, we are dust – mortal – and one day we will return to dust. Which is why the psalmist says, *"Teach us to number our days, so we may gain a heart of wisdom"* – so we may never take our lives for granted or waste the precious time we've been given.

I told him that the ashes remind us to live fully who we are without trying to make ourselves to be more than we are or less than we are. The ashes invite us to become "grounded," to live with humility (from the Latin *humus* – soil, ground) so that the best of things grow in us.

The ashes also remind us we are, each of us, marked with something gritty that is uncomfortable and unsightly. Our sin leaves us broken, and our brokenness is sometimes as visible as the mark on our foreheads.

But no matter how mortal or how broken, God still loves us and God still sees in us something sacred. So while we are marked by these ashes, we are marked with a cross – with a sign of hope, with the sign that Christ Himself claims us as His own and now walks with us.

Doug is a minister. He knows these things; he speaks some form of these thoughts often. But when I finished, he looked at me with wide eyes and excitement and said, "That is awesome!"

I think that is what it means to pray for forgiveness – to receive it and to give it to others. For as I marked Doug, I could see that, despite my words, it was my dirty finger that had smudged his forehead. I need his forgiveness and God's forgiveness because of the marks

I leave on others and for the marks others have left on me, these dirty smears that painfully remind us of those times we have tried to rise above the lower elements of our life only to sink deeper in the dirt.

So we ask for and we give forgiveness so that we can share the awesome word that love is more potent than hate, that hope is greater than despair, and that life is stronger than death.

"And lead us not into temptation, but deliver us from evil."

She was the first person who came to me after I began my shift. Catholic by background, she and her husband – a Baptist – had found the warmth and love of First Presbyterian Church to be the ideal middle ground for their family's faith. She was thrilled when she heard we would be sharing the ashes during the daytime hours because her work obligations would prevent her from attending the evening service at First Presbyterian that evening. Ash Wednesday was something that re-connected her to her Catholic roots as well as her Hispanic culture.

Though I am a stranger to her, she is friendly and trusting of me because her pastor says she can trust what his colleagues would share with her. So she comes with remarkable faith – faith in God, faith in Ted, and now, even faith in me. She marks me with a grace I did not deserve.

And in turn, I mark her with ashes. She is young, the mother of two preschoolers, so to mark her and remind her she is mortal seems such a harsh word for someone so full of life. Yet she closes her eyes and trusts me to touch her forehead and mark her with mortality for all to see.

And then, with joy, she responds back with gratitude. She embodies the ashes – she is mortal – as well as the promise of this day. Her face reflects her determination to live fully each moment she has left, numbering her days with a heart of wisdom. Then off she goes to work with the peace of Christ being more than words that I have spoken to her. They are words that clearly reign in her heart.

So when I think of this woman who trusts me, and of others like her – my colleagues, friends in our church's family of faith, my own wife, no less – when I think of all these people in my life, I begin to understand why Jesus closes with words about temptation, about failing a test of character and will. Of yielding to something that would break that trust. My actions have implications far beyond my own life. So I pray for the strength to live in a way that never breaks their trust, that never lowers their view of God or of the cross that marks my forehead.

"Pray this way…"

This is the prayer I began praying today at *Starbucks*. And it is what I want to do this season – to learn to pray in this way every day and to live in this way so that that God's will in Heaven might be done on earth and in me.

This is the Ash Wednesday Gospel according to *Starbucks*. Thanks be to God. Amen.

———

This reflection was composed from notes taken at Starbucks on Wednesday, March 5, 2014, and adapted for a community Lenten Lunch series on Thursday, March 13, 2014.

"The Season of Simplicity"

*"Do not store up for yourselves treasures on earth, where moth
and rust consume and where thieves break in and steal; 20but
store up for yourselves treasures in heaven, where neither moth nor
rust consumes and where thieves do not break in and steal. 21For
where your treasure is, there your heart will be also."*

Matthew 6:19-21, *New Revised Standard Version*

As with the last couple of years, my reflection tonight was greatly influenced by the *"Ashes to Go"* experience I shared with colleagues today at *Starbucks*.

I arrived around 10:00 this morning and was greeted by Doug from First Baptist Church. Which was really interesting because last year was his first time *ever* to participate in an Ash Wednesday experience. But he wanted to give it a try and he came away deeply moved by it. So he was the first to sign up this year.

Last year I had shared with him some of the words I used to impart the ashes. This year, he told me, it was his turn to do the same to me. "It is both bad news and good news," he began. The bad news was found in the sobering words about being a sinner and under the cloud of death; the good news was God's love in Christ that forgives my sins and offers me new life.

I noticed he spoke those words with enthusiasm. With joy in his eyes he marked my forehead with the sign of the cross, offering me words of grace and hope and assurance.

It was so simple – and yet so profound.

I think that is why I enjoy Ash Wednesday and this season of Lent so much – its simplicity. In intimate face-to-face conversations, in a few simple but personal words, and in the touch of acceptance and grace we experience the essence of the Good News.

During this season, we allow Jesus' words to lead us back to the practice of a simple faith:

> – simplicity in giving, keeping the focus on the person receiving the gift rather that what we gave or how we gave it;

> – simplicity in praying, using words that are real and honest, personal and intimate that express our need for God, our concern for loved ones and neighbors, and even our hopes for our enemies;

> – simplicity in fasting, choosing to go without food or an activity in order to make space for God and the people around us to come into our lives in a deeper way.

My first guest walked into *Starbucks* and, as he headed for the restroom, glanced over at me.

A few minutes later he came over to me and said that when he saw me and the ashes on my forehead that it reminded him it was Ash Wednesday and he was going to give up coffee for Lent! He sat down and I shared a few simple words and marked his forehead with an ashen cross, and then off he went – empty-handed but perhaps full-hearted.

You see, Lent invites us to renew our faith, to make room again in our lives for the simplest things that bring God's love to us in new ways.

We start with the ashes, with the remains of a prior year's Palm Sunday branches. Those ashes reflect our own stories – the hopes that went sour, the relationships that broke down, the moments when our best intentions failed, the moments when we had no intentions at all. In a hundred ways we are already marked by the ashes of loss of those things that died in us or around us. And we already know that these are the things that separate us from God and others and ourselves.

And yet in imposing the ashes, a hand reaches across the separation and bridges the gap. We touch and in that simple act of grace we breathe a deep sigh of relief that whatever has happened to separate us does not have to keep us apart.

That's why we use the cross. It rises like a phoenix out of the ashes of loss. For it was "while we were yet sinners" that Christ died for us. The cross is the undying sign of God's love for us, that nothing from the past changes the fact we are God's children and we belong to Him.

Invitation to the Lenten Discipline

So I invite you into the simplicity of this season to rediscover this grace, to allow it to mark you not only on your forehead but in your heart.

During the next 40 days, we are invited to spend more time reading the Bible, praying, reflecting, and engaging in intentional times of silence, solitude and service.

We're also invited to the discipline of fasting — purposefully going without something meaningful to us as an offering to God. During this season, we choose to give up some food or activity – television, music, the internet, etc. – and go without it for a period of time (40 days, except Sundays – a grace day!).

The reason? So that, each time you think of this thing you've given to God instead of yourself, it will remind you to invite God to come into that place where you have made room so God can truly fill you.

These simple spiritual habits can have an amazing effect on us. They can help renew your understanding of God's love for you and the joy of God's grace in your life. This is the Ash Wednesday Gospel according to *Starbucks*. Thanks be to God. Amen.

————

This reflection was composed from notes taken at Starbucks on Wednesday, February 18, 2015.

"Whenever You Pray..."

*"And whenever you pray, do not be like the hypocrites; for they love to
stand and pray in the synagogues and at the street corners, so that they
may be seen by others.
Truly I tell you, they have received their reward.
6But whenever you pray, go into your room and shut the door and
pray to your Father who is in secret; and your Father who sees in secret
will reward you.*

*7"When you are praying, do not heap up empty phrases as the Gentiles
do; for they think that they will be heard because of their many words.
8Do not be like them, for your Father knows what you need before you
ask him. 9Pray then in this way:
Our Father in heaven, hallowed be your name.*

*10Your kingdom come. Your will be done, on earth as it is in heaven.
11Give us this day our daily bread.
12And forgive us our debts, as we also have forgiven our debtors.
13And do not bring us to the time of trial, but rescue us from the evil
one. For the kingdom and the power and the glory are yours forever.
Amen."*

Matthew 6:5-13, *New Revised Standard Edition*

———

Jesus' prayer will be our guide throughout the Season of
Lent. Each Sunday we will reflect on one of the phrases
of this prayer and allow it to shape both how we
understand prayer and how we actually pray.

These words shaped my prayers at *Starbucks* this
morning as I shared with my colleagues in the "ashes to
go" ministry. As in the past three years, my reflection

for tonight was shaped by what happened this morning and the thoughts I wrote in my journal.

I arrive for my 10:00-12:00 shift and am greeted by "Mother" Mary Erickson, rector of the Episcopal Church of the Ascension. She welcomes me with warmth and we sit down like good friends and talk about the latest happenings in our lives – words that are a kind of sacred liturgy in and of themselves.

That's when it strikes me that such conversations are one of the most compelling images I have of prayer – meeting with someone and talking with and listening to them and sharing with them things that are personal and important. This is how Jesus describes prayer – no street corner performances, but a quiet meeting over a cup of coffee; something intimate and personal, something that nourishes and restores the soul in the same way friendship does.

Mary and I speak of the busyness of our lives. She listens in a way that is unhurried. I find her to be such a person of peace, a very "non-anxious" presence.

We begin the Ash Wednesday ritual as if it is simply part of our conversation as friends. As she speaks the truth to me that I am dust and mortal, she marks me with ashes but does so with pastoral tenderness as if it pains her to tell me such truth. Then she speaks the words of hope – words about God's love, words about God's forgiveness, words about new life. It is the counterbalance to the heaviness of our mortality. We offer each other the peace of Christ, and then, as she leaves, Mary places the ritual into my hands to carry on with others.

The first person to seek me out turns out to be a woman from Church of the Ascension. Her work will keep her from sharing in her own church's Ash Wednesday service that evening, so she comes to *Starbucks* to begin her day. She does not know me, but because she trusts "Mother Mary" she trusts me and sits expectantly across from me. I am reminded that we are family, for we both begin our prayers with *"Our Father..."* So here we sit, a brother and sister in God's family.

As I place the ashes on her forehead, I remind her that she, too, is mortal. I also note that the ashes speak of another sobering truth – that our fear of our mortality causes us to mark each other in ways that often are as visible as the ashes she and I both wear this day. *"Forgive us our sins, dear Father, as we forgive those who sin against us."*

But then comes my chance to offer words of Good News – the hope that we are marked by a cross, by the sign of God's love in Christ that makes possible a new life and a new way of life. She smiles and with a benediction of peace she goes on her way.

A few minutes later, my friend and Heritage church member, Bird LeCroy, arrives, looking good after his recent heart attack. Dressed in a denim jacket with some *Grateful Dead* patches sewn on it, he makes me smile. He feels good today, he tells me, and this is his longest outing since being discharged from the hospital.

We talk for a bit and then I reach out to mark his forehead with ashes. He knows the truth that we are mortal all too well, and it is painful to think how close he came to death. But now he sits before me as the grateful *almost* dead!

The cross reminds us both of our hope – that God has stepped into our dust and with love has redeemed us, has rescued us. As he leaves, Bird embodies the joy of that news, so full of gratitude and deeply aware of the gift of life and the fresh start he has received.

Almost at the same time, three more people arrive. I try to offer the words of truth and hope in an unhurried way; I do not wish to rush this ritual lest I dilute its meaning and contradict its invitation to pause and ponder not only on this day but throughout this season.

Friend and fellow church member Pat McCoy sits down, but then a woman behind her interrupts. She looks both anxious and expectant as she earnestly says, "I _need_ to receive the ashes." Pat stands up and steps away to get coffee. The woman takes her seat across from me. Her name is Mary, and like her biblical namesake she is quiet. As I share with her words of repentance and hope, I pray that the sign of the cross on her forehead will remind her throughout the day that the One she seeks is with her, and that she will find her needs met. *"Give us both this day our daily bread."*

Pat returns with coffee and we talk for a few minutes before I begin with the ashes. As someone who has come back from cancer, she knows all too well she is mortal. But she also knows the incredible power of love to conquer fear and death itself. Her physical scars are no match for the mark of hope she will wear throughout this day.

As Pat leaves, my wife, Vicki, sits down across from me. I tell her that with the rash of funerals I've performed in the past several weeks, it gives me pause to mark her with a sign of mortality. The thought of losing her

34

leaves me with a pit in my stomach as I press my ashen fingers to her forehead and speak those haunting words about being dust. And then, as I trace the cross with those ashes, I see in them the sign of what is both her hope and mine – that God's love will persist and prevail in all things. For love is stronger than death. *"For thine is the kingdom and the power and the glory, forever. Amen."*

With a kiss she steps away from me, already thinking of how she can do something nice for the woman she is going to see. *"Thy kingdom come, thy will be done in earth as it is in heaven."* I give thanks for all the ways she embodies the hope and the grace of God.

As Vicki leaves, a woman named Kathy, also from Church of the Ascension, sits down across from me. I assure her I do not kiss everyone who receives the ashes today! She laughs, and then I begin to mark her with the ashes. I describe how they serve as both a sign of mortality and a sign of our brokenness, which is often displayed in ways that are as visible as the mark I leave upon her forehead.

She looks somewhat startled by my words, perhaps because this Baptist doesn't stick to the precise words of the ritual with which she is more familiar. *"Forgive us our trespasses..."!*

Then I tell her that we are marked with the cross – that no matter how mortal or how broken, God still loves us; God still sees in us something sacred. So though we are marked by ashes, they are traced in the form of a cross – with the sign of hope, with the sign that Christ Himself became dust and was nearly reduced to dust, but by walking in our shoes God has redeemed us from being *only* dust.

Again with something of a startled look she replies, "That's awesome!"

I urge her to go with hope into her day, and that each time she sees the cross on her forehead or each time another person sees it, she and they might know that it is a sign of God's redeeming love. "I like that," she says, repeating the words, "redeeming love."

"May the peace of Christ be with you," I say. "And also with you," she replies.

A few minutes later, Kirk Bozeman from Trinity United Methodist comes to pick up the mantel and share the message of hope for the next hour. I share words similar to what I've shared with others throughout the past two hours and mark his forehead. "That's a good word," he says. We extend the peace of Christ to each other, and then I leave.

What does all that have to do with the Lord's Prayer?

"Our Father..." begins the Lord's Prayer. My morning in the coffee shop made me very aware that the One to whom I pray is the Father of all who sat at that table with me today in Starbucks, and even of those who simply passed through that place. For each of us, friends and strangers alike, all turn to the Father when we are in need,
- when we are searching, when we are hurt,
- when we need forgiveness, when we face temptation,
- when the very essence of who we are is tested by the issues we face,
- and when our lives are so full of joy that we cannot help but end our prayers with praise.

"Our Father..." Just thinking of those words drives home the notion that I – we – *each* of us are connected to the larger Body of Christ in the world and in our community. And that each time I/we pray the prayer Jesus taught, I/we never do so alone. We are joined by "Mother" Mary and Bird; by the woman who's name I can't remember and by Pat; by Kathy and the other Mary; by Vicki and by Kirk; by the *Starbucks* employee who goes out of her way to help a young mother toting her infant and preschooler; and by all who breathe the same air and share the same common ground created by our Father in heaven.

"Hallowed be Thy name..." In sharing together, in finding ways to work and witness together, in listening to each other, in caring about one another and helping one another find our daily bread, in asking for and extending forgiveness to one another, in sharing courage and encouragement with each other when we would just as soon throw in the towel and quit – that such things not only bear witness to our one Father, but it seems to me that in doing these things we are, in fact, hallowing God's name. We cause the name of God to become greater and more important to us, which perhaps is the only way it also will become greater and more important to others.

So when I live this way with my brothers and sisters – when I take time to *see* them and *serve* them as my brothers and sisters – it helps me more clearly understand that the Kingdom of God I pray will one day come is, in many ways, already here, waiting only on me to open my eyes to it and welcome it and share it so that God's will done in heaven might also be done in the earth – and in me.

"Pray this way..." Jesus says before He teaches us His prayer.

What happened for me and others at *Starbucks* points me in the direction of what I think He had in mind. For whether we use His words or words of our own, whenever we "pray this way" – this eyes-open, heart-open way – we shall find ourselves connecting with God and one another in powerful ways, enriching ways.

That is what I want to do this season – to learn to pray this way. Would you join me? This is the Ash Wednesday Gospel according to *Starbucks*. Thanks be to God. Amen.

———

This reflection was composed from notes taken at Starbucks on Wednesday, February 10, 2016, and adapted for a community Lenten Lunch series on Thursday, February 18, 2016.

"The Heart of the Matter"

I've been out of step with you for a long time, in the wrong since before I was born. 6What you're after is truth from the inside out. Enter me, then; conceive a new, true life. 7Soak me in your laundry and I'll come out clean, scrub me and I'll have a snow-white life.

8Tune me in to foot-tapping songs, set these once-broken bones to dancing. 9Don't look too close for blemishes, give me a clean bill of health.

10God, make a fresh start in me, shape a Genesis week from the chaos of my life.

Psalm 51:5-10, *The Message*

Create in me a clean heart, O God, and put a new and right spirit within me.

Psalm 51:10, *New Revised Standard Version*

One of the teachers of religious law was standing there listening to the debate. He realized that Jesus had answered well, so he asked, "Of all the commandments, which is the most important?"

29Jesus replied, "The most important commandment is this: 'Listen, O Israel! The LORD our God is the one and only LORD. 30And you must love the LORD your God with all your heart, all your soul, all your mind, and all your strength.' 31The second is equally important: 'Love your neighbor as yourself.' No other commandment is greater than these."

32The teacher of religious law replied, "Well said, Teacher. You have spoken the truth by saying that there is only one God and no other. 33And I know it is important to love him with all my heart and all my understanding and all my strength, and to love my neighbor as myself. This is more important than to offer all of the burnt offerings and sacrifices required in the law."

34Realizing how much the man understood, Jesus said to him, "You are not far from the Kingdom of God."

And after that, no one dared to ask him any more questions.

Mark 12:28-34, *New Living Translation*

———————

As with the last couple of years, my reflections for this evening were shaped by the *"Ashes to Go"* experience I shared with colleagues today at *Starbucks*. From 7:00 a.m. until 1:30, a handful of us took shifts and marked those who wished it with ashes.

This is the first time in over half a century that Valentine's Day has fallen on Ash Wednesday. The fact that today's ancient tradition also fell on Valentine's Day also played into my thoughts for tonight, as well as the theme for this Lenten season. *"The Heart of the Matter."*

We say those words when we wish to get at the essence of something, the bottom line of an issue. It reflects something vital, the focal point of a topic or problem. We sometimes use the phrase "the crux" of the matter – an old word for "cross," which is the primary symbol for Ash Wednesday and for the Lenten season. The cross gives us the image of where two things meet, where they connect – God and humanity; sin and mercy; death and life.

So what is the heart of the matter behind Ash Wednesday, and behind the next six weeks of this season of Lent as we journey with Jesus toward the cross and the empty tomb? My time at *Starbucks* helped me see the heart of the matter more clearly.

I have come to love this Ash Wednesday tradition at *Starbucks*, this time of engaging with people one-on-one and talking personally about the mystery of God's love. Then, in the silence in between guests, I write about the people who come and what we share. I developed the practice of allowing my Ash Wednesday reflection to flow from these notes. Though it seems last minute to wait until late in that day to start writing, I do not find myself anxious about finding the right words or feeling like I have to say something "profound." I come with a sense that God will speak if I will but take the time to listen. And God does.

I arrived at 9:00 a.m. this morning and was greeted by Mary from Church of the Ascension. We spend some time just "catching up." We speak of family and of a book she has been reading that is shaping her thoughts about Lent. Written more than a century ago, she finds the book offers some fresh perspective on the word *metanoia*. It's most commonly translated into English as "repent," but that doesn't nearly capture the depth of meaning behind the Greek word. It involves a whole re-orientation of mind, body and soul. More than a turning away from something, it also means turning toward something that captivates us and changes the way we see everything. And then, we begin to live and walk toward that new light.

After all this talk of life and light, she then marks me with the ashes of death. Her words are simple and sobering: *"You are dust."*

Dust. Frail. Mortal. No need to be reminded of this truth as two church members lay in hospice care this week. They are both advanced in age, yet I suspect each of them as well as their families, sense that the time has flown by. Who knew the end could and would *really* come?

"You are dust." Though she does not speak it, in my mind I add the words, *"So repent and believe the Gospel."* Allow this truth to awaken you to the value of this time and choose to live fully, passionately.

As Mary is leaving, Ben, an acquaintance I have not seen for a while, stops by. We chat for a minute and I ask if he would like to have the ashes. He is unfamiliar with what it means and sits down to listen as this Baptist tries to explain this ancient Catholic/Christian tradition!

Ashes have been used for centuries as a symbol of something serious, I begin. We recognize something that stops us in our tracks and makes us take a hard look at our lives and the path we're walking. With the ashes we hear a hard truth – we are dust, we are mortal. And if mortal – *if we shall truly die* – then how do we want to live? With ashes of regret or sorrow, we turn toward that better path.

I conclude by saying that while we mark ourselves with ashes – with this stark, in-your-face reminder that we also are dust – we do so with the sign of the cross, the symbol of God's determination to reclaim us from being *merely* dust.

"Would you like the ashes, then?" I ask. And eagerly he agrees. As he walks away, I think how that sign will be visible to him for the rest of the day each time he looks in the mirror, or someone asks him what is on his forehead. And I wonder how it will change his day.

Within a few minutes, a man named Eric sees me and recognizes what I'm doing. An Episcopalian who cannot make his own church's service in Marietta, he is grateful for the opportunity to receive the ashes. I do not bother to tell him I am Baptist. Some things are better left unsaid.

We talk for a few minutes and his joy and energy are infectious. When I remind him we are marked with the sign of God's love, he immediately responds, "Absolutely! Love – that's what it's all about." I send him off with a hug and the peace of Christ, reminding him to repent – to remember and live with this truth of love and believe it. He looks at me and says seriously, "I will. I *will* try to believe that."

Stan comes a few minutes later. He is also full of energy, and since we have met before in the community, he asks how I've been and how things are going at the church. I am struck by his thoughtfulness, and by how personal these encounters are each year. Unhurried conversations, deep connections in a short amount of time. In these brief moments in the coffee shop, we take time to look one another in the eye and truly *see* one another with more than a passing glance and listen deeply to one another. And then I think about the trust it takes for him and the others today to allow me to touch their foreheads and smear them with gritty ash.

No sooner does Stan leave than a young couple, Andy and Amanda, come to the table. I find myself liking them instantly. They are open and interested – and interesting. He tells me he was raised as a Catholic, though his grandmother was a "hard" Tennessee Baptist who at the same time was full of grace. He is familiar with the Ash Wednesday tradition and is eager to share in it. It is, he says, something he "needs."

Amanda is Baptist by background, so the idea of receiving the ashes is new to her. Yet it is also deeply appealing. She adds that they have wanted to find a church for themselves and for their 17-year-old daughter. Stopping to do this together seems to have awakened that need again and created a new sense of urgency for them.

I introduce myself and when they ask about my church, I give them my standard line: "I am Baptist – but I'm just not mad about it!" They both laugh and relax even more. When they ask where the church is, I tell them that we are the Baptist church on the *left side* of Douthit Ferry Road, and they laugh again.

As I mark them with the cross and speak about the meaning of what we're doing together, they drink it in. They both say how much they have needed this, how they are glad they stopped. They want their daughter to see the marks on their foreheads and be able to tell her why they did it in hopes of helping her think about God and her own faith in some way.

They go to join a friend elsewhere in the coffee shop, but soon Amanda returns and shares more deeply some concerns for her daughter. No problems, just a recognition that she has choices ahead of her and wants her to find a good path for her life. She speaks of how her daughter confides in her – even with things that parents sometimes wish they didn't know! I commend her for creating the kind of trust that allows her daughter to do that and affirm her for listening to her daughter in a way that tells her she values what she is saying. Amanda breathes a deep sigh and says, "It's going to be all right, isn't it." I assure her it will be, and that she is a good mother.

She goes back to join Andy and their friend, but as they leave, they stop by the table for one more hug. They ask more about the church and our community ministries. As they leave, they tell me that they hope to see me this coming Sunday.

My good friend and fellow church member Bird has been patiently waiting in the background. He knows something sacred has been happening, so he quietly waited and now comes to the table to join me. He also shares concerns about friends and family. I am struck by how deeply he feels for other people and how he so willingly seeks to lessen the weight that others carry. He speaks about his awareness of God's grace in everything – something that surprises even him. Five years ago, he tells me, he was in a different place. Had he been told then where he would be now in his faith he would not have believed it. His gratitude for re-discovering and re-engaging with his faith spills over us. As I mark his forehead, I am aware of my own gratitude for his friendship, his passion, his joy – all gifts that he readily shares with so many people. He is my pony-tailed, *Grateful Dead*-loving brother who enriches me each and every time we spend time together!

Surprisingly, more than two hours have passed since I began the morning when Doug arrives for his shift. I share how meaningful the morning has been for me, and our conversation is icing on the cake. I find it amusing that it will be two Baptists who will offer the last words at *Starbucks* about the Ash Wednesday tradition that neither of us grew up knowing or practicing! God surely has a sense of humor.

He leans in as I begin to remind him of the hard truth that we are dust – we are mortal – smearing the ashes on his forehead. I also remind him that the Lenten season begins under the shadow of the cross. When Jesus makes the turn in His ministry toward Jerusalem, He understands what is coming. He faces a rendezvous with His own mortality.

Yet knowing His remaining time is brief, the Bible shows how He lives in light of that truth. Along the way, He will respond to people with incredible compassion and care. He will perform some amazing miracles, and His teaching will offer profound insights on what it means to love God and love others. With His closest friends, He will create meaningful memories that will allow them to recall His actions and words for the rest of their lives. He will even find a way to forgive those who treat Him shamefully and brutally. He will pour Himself out until His last breath, holding nothing back but giving Himself in love to others.

So we mark ourselves with ashes – the reminder that we also are dust – but we do so with the sign of the cross, reminding us of the greater truth that though we are dust, God believes we are *sacred* dust. With the cross, we are marked with the sign of God's love and the hope that, while we are mortal, love is stronger than death.

"THAT," he says smiling, "is really Good News!"

My morning at *Starbucks* reminds me anew that it is this Good News that is the heart of the matter of our faith.

It is why the cross, whether traced with ash on our foreheads or dangling from a necklace close to our heart, appeals so deeply to us. For the cross has the power to awaken in us something that we long for and something that we long to become.

It will not be until later that day that I learn of the Florida high school shooting. And the picture that will lead the news articles will show a woman in tears, a large cross of ashes on her forehead, embracing another woman in tears outside of that school.

Young lives cut short. *Ashes to ashes, dust to dust.*

Yet, in the midst of that fear and sorrow and grief, there is the cross. Simple homemade white crosses with the names of students cut down in their classrooms. Now surrounded by flowers as mourners come to remember.

The cross. The sign of God's dogged determination to find a way to stand with us in the worst that happens. The sign that even when we do the worst to one another and to God Himself, there is a grace that will meet us there so that the worst thing that might happen to us will never be the last thing that happens to us.

This is the Good News from *Starbucks*. Repent, and believe this Good News. And may it re-shape everything we think and say and do each day, every day, all of our days. Amen.

———

This reflection was compiled from journal notes made on Ash Wednesday, February 14, 2018, and adapted for a community Lenten Lunch reflection shared on Thursday, February 22, 2018.

"Mercy"

Have mercy on me, O God, because of your unfailing love. Because of your great compassion, blot out the stain of my sins. 2Wash me clean from my guilt. Purify me from my sin.

3For I recognize my shameful deeds — they haunt me day and night.

4Against you, and you alone, have I sinned; I have done what is evil in your sight. You will be proved right in what you say, and your judgment against me is just. 5For I was born a sinner — yes, from the moment my mother conceived me.

6But you desire honesty from the heart, so you can teach me to be wise in my inmost being. 7Purify me from my sins, and I will be clean; wash me, and I will be whiter than snow.

8Oh, give me back my joy again; you have broken me — now let me rejoice. 9Don't keep looking at my sins. Remove the stain of my guilt.

10Create in me a clean heart, O God. Renew a right spirit within me. 11Do not banish me from your presence, and don't take your Holy Spirit from me.

12Restore to me again the joy of your salvation, and make me willing to obey you. 13Then I will teach your ways to sinners, and they will return to you. 14Forgive me for shedding blood, O God who saves; then I will joyfully sing of your forgiveness.

Psalms 51:1-3,10-13 *New Living Translation, Second Edition*

"Pray then in this way: Our Father in heaven, hallowed be your name. 10Your kingdom come. Your will be done, on earth as it is in heaven.

11Give us this day our daily bread. 12And forgive us our debts, as we also have forgiven our debtors."

Matthew 6:1-18, *New Revised Standard Version*

Clergy friends and I shared *"Ashes to Go"* in a local coffee shop again today. For the past several years, we've been at *Starbucks*. This year we opted for *Noble and Main*, a relatively new coffee shop that renovated an old service station and is now serving up high-octane coffee.

I was struck by all the young adults who came through the shop. With the modern industrial look – concrete floor with acid treatment; contemporary art; simple, cleaned-line tables – it has a kind of "hip" vibe to it. Which made me feel instantly old. The only thing "hip" about me is the one made of titanium in my left thigh.

"Remember you are dust, and to dust you shall return." The young people coming in and out rub that reality in my face long before the ashes are placed there.

I find Doug waiting for me. Another Baptist, he has taken the 2-hour shift prior to mine and he greets me warmly. He points to a nearby table of women, all with ashen crosses on their foreheads. And he says that all of them were celebrating Ash Wednesday for the first time in their Baptist lives!

He and I then sit down and talk about families, our work, our lives. And then he prepares to pass the responsibility for sharing the ashes by marking my forehead.

As he does so, he tells me a story. It's the tale of two kingdoms, he begins. And he goes on to describe the first as a kingdom of darkness and brokenness. It is the world we know so well, too well. Yet into this world steps Jesus, whose Kingdom is one of light and grace and hope. His death and resurrection open the door to His Kingdom, which we can experience even in this world.

He marks me with the ashes, the gritty reality of my day-to-day world. And then he offers me the words of assurance – that the ashes are in the shape of a cross, the sign of God's unrelenting love for this world, and determination to bring us out of the darkness and into the light.

We hug goodbye, grateful to see one another (it's been a while) and grateful for each other. I take his place at the table, and within moments a steady stream of people begin to arrive. Among the first is Lee, the chaplain I first met two weeks ago. A power outage on a cold January day had shut down the Hickory Log group home for developmentally challenged men. They came and took refuge at the church for a day until power was restored. She tells me a handful of the residents are coming to the shop, and as we speak the van pulls up and they begin to get out.

I recognize some of the men from their visit with us; a few of them recognize me. I watch Lee and Terry, the manager, patiently work with them on their orders of coffee or hot chocolate and cookies. While they tend to their flock, Terry's father – visiting from Cleveland, Ohio – sits down with me. He speaks of his faith, of the challenges to his faith, and then invites me to mark his forehead.

The men from the group home sit as a group at a nearby table, and a couple of the men want to have the ashes on their foreheads, too. I do so and offer a short prayer with each of them.

Then Terry and Lee each take turns receiving the ashes. I remind them how the ashes are an ancient symbol for repentance as well as a reminder of our mortality. *"You more than most,"* I tell them, *"understand how frail we are, how broken we can be in both body and soul."* Yet into our frail and broken lives, God sends Jesus, I remind them. And His love redeems us and heals the brokenness. The cross serves as our reminder that love is stronger than the worst that is in us or around us. Love is even stronger than death. Powerful words, especially for Terry whose husband Scott died two years ago.

She returns to help gather up the men. We all say our goodbyes and the group shuffles out.

As I turn, I see a woman sitting in the corner. She has been waiting for the crowd to clear so she can receive the ashes. When she comes to the table I thank her for her patience. She confesses she may have looked so on the outside but was far from it on the inside! We talk for a few minutes and then I mark her with the sign of the cross and offer her a blessing for the season ahead.

A couple of strangers come to the table, receive the ashes gratefully, and leave. And then friends – Jeremy North and then later, Bird – come by, each of them lingering so we can talk at length. I mark their foreheads, speaking those sobering words of death and life, of frailty and possibility.

Vicki is one of the last to come during my shift. Marking my wife with words about life's brevity is sobering for me. Yet the ashen cross carries with it the promise that, like a phoenix, we shall rise to new life through the power of God's love.

My shift ends with one more stranger. She had been waiting by the counter with her cup and as Vicki leaves she makes her way to the table. As I mark her forehead and remind her of the hope that the cross is stronger than death itself, she seizes my hands in gratitude and offers me a blessing before leaving.

Throughout the day, David's words from Psalm 51 have been in the back of my mind. *"Have mercy on me, O God..."* And it seems that is what we all share in coming to the coffee shop. A longing for mercy, for some word of hope. We come because we know that there are parts of our lives that are as gritty and grimy as the ash on our foreheads. And our sins don't just affect us; we *infect* one another. It is as if the ash on our foreheads is also on our fingers, and we realize that we mark and mar each other with our sin.

On Ash Wednesday, we decide to look at it. Allow it to confront us. Haunt us. But also challenge us. For, like David, we are invited to bring ourselves into the light of God's love. We may do so fearfully, like approaching a stranger in a coffee shop. But then we discover that God desires to release us from the burden of guilt and shame that plague us. The good news is that God loves us and longs to forgive us and free us to live the lives we were intended to live.

That's what is at the heart of this season – forgiveness and freedom, renewal and resurrection.

Whatever "sin" stands as an obstacle to our search for God, our reconciliation with others, or the healing for ourselves is as close as the tender hand that traces a cross on our foreheads.

It's a reminder that the only thing that can ever overcome guilt is love. The love of others who see us for what we are, know us for what we've done, and still welcome us. The love of God that knows this about us, too, and as Doug reminded me today, "Even while we were still sinners, Christ died for us."

When I went to mark each person today, I became aware that each face I touched was unique; I stared into eyes deep with longing, faces that bore the marks of joys and sorrows and regrets. And in each face was the longing for someone to tell them they were more than dust.

Which is why the ashes of this day mark us with the cross, reminding us one more time when we stare in the mirror to wash our faces tonight that it is the cross that lifts us out of the dust.

The cross – the instrument of death – turns out to be a sign of life:

- a sign that grace is greater than guilt,
- that hope is more powerful than despair,
- that love is stronger than death.

This is the hope we all have –
    to love and to be loved;
    to share ourselves with another;
    to find a connection that makes us feel like we are
        more than dust;
    to hear a word that allows us to become more than
        dust.

This is the Ash Wednesday Gospel from the hip coffee shop on Main Street. Thanks be to God. Amen.

———

This Ash Wednesday reflection was written from notes made at Noble and Main Coffee Shop on March 6, 2019.

"Renewing the Heart"

You desire honesty from the heart, so you can teach me to be wise in my inmost being. 7Purify me from my sins, and I will be clean; wash me, and I will be whiter than snow. 8Oh, give me back my joy again; you have broken me — now let me rejoice. 9Don't keep looking at my sins. Remove the stain of my guilt. 10Create in me a clean heart, O God. Renew a right spirit within me.

Psalms 51:6-10, *New Living Translation, Second Edition*

Much of my reflection this year comes again from today's experience of *"Ashes to Go."* Like last year, we clergy set up at *Noble and Main*, the relatively new place in town that converted an old service station into a high-octane coffee shop.

I left the house in a hurry, all flustered this morning. I had tried to squeeze one more thing into the morning before leaving. It wound up taking more time than I had allowed. Of course. So I drove to the shop preoccupied and irritated. (Slow drivers always wait to get on the road right before people who run late.) I wrote in my journal that it was a nice attitude to take on the way to "being spiritual."

Once there, even in the busyness of the shop, I received the first gift of this Lenten season – peace, quiet. Time unhurried. Time for listening.

Young folks walk in and out all morning during my 9-11 shift – all smiles, some laughter as they are greeting one another. It is the "place to be" apparently if you're young. I am old and immediately feel out of place. *"Remember you are dust, and to dust you shall return."* I am reminded anew how much closer I am to that reality than the young people around me.

There is a lot, however, that we share in common. They offer something similar to what I am offering – grace, acceptance, the gift of being valued. They take their place at tables around me. The sound of their voices suggests their conversations are serious, important. Like this day is.

None of them has asked for ashes for their foreheads, though. Yet the mark of concern they have for each other is as visible on their faces and in the expressions as any cross they might wear.

When I first arrived, three women had just come to receive ashes. Cathy – a member at Ascension whom I have marked in previous years – and two others who are together. Mother Mary, as she is affectionately called at Ascension, warmly greets each one, speaks quietly to them, and then marks them with dark ashen crosses that will be obvious throughout the rest of their day. I watch and wait from a distance.

Then I take a seat at Mary's table. We have a few minutes to catch up together. She's looking forward to an extended visit from her daughter and son-in-law out west. Her other children will come in for part of the time, too – a family reunion of sorts apart from a holiday. She is already relishing the thought of having all her chicks under wing and plans to take time off to be with them in this busy church season.

When she is ready to go, she marks me with the ash and

I do the same to her. The sobering words about mortality now are written on our foreheads for all to see. She offers a parting thought – wondering aloud whether the coronavirus might lead to empty churches at Easter if people are forced to quarantine themselves. *"Remember you are dust, and to dust you shall return."* Ominous words for our fragile world.

By 10:00 a.m. the shop is bustling. No takers for ashes, however. When I take a quick bathroom break, I catch sight of my forehead in the mirror. Mary marked me well – looks like she used a Sharpie instead of ashes! Certainly no mistaking what day it is.

A couple of young mothers come in with their infant and toddler children. They glance my way but don't stop. What mother ever wants to think of her child's mortality?

Beth arrives and immediately seeks me out. She is full of energy as usual. We chat for a few minutes and then I trace the cross in ash on her forehead. She is quiet, and speaks, "I've been thinking about death a lot lately," she says thoughtfully. She speaks of someone nearing death, and of losses in her own family this past year. And then she speaks of her own belief that death is not the end. "Ash always leads back to fire," I tell her. God's love is the fire that makes all things new. A reminder there is always hope in the face of loss.

She later tells me that at lunch, one of her Catholic friends said she knew she was not going to have time to go by her own church today to receive the ashes. So she lifted Beth's hair, rubbed ashes from her forehead and then placed them on her own! Leave it to the Baptists to make Ash Wednesday possible for the Catholics!

After Beth leaves, a young man sitting behind me asks if I am Catholic. Drew is his name, and he is surprised when I tell him I am Baptist. It opens the door to talk about the tradition behind the ashes and the Lenten season. A Baptist himself, it is all new to him. He then shares that he's leading a student Bible study later at the Georgia Highland campus. It started with a single student and now has grown to a dozen. Though he declined to receive ashes, he does ask that I pray for his study later at 3:30.

Young adults come and go throughout the morning. Most seem to be students and the shop has become a place for study. At most they cast a sideways glance my way but they don't register much if any interest. It's unclear whether they have no interest in this tradition or whether they have no interest in anything "religious."

And yet, this coffee shop has become something of a sanctuary to them. I hear some of them speak about how often they are there or how long it has been since one of their friends has come by at the same time. It's clear that they come here for more than coffee. They come here because it has become a sacred place for them. Sacred things happen to them when they gather in this space with friends. They become more themselves because of the grace they receive from each other. Like David, their spirit is restored and a new and right heart begins to beat in them again.

Like most of us, they may not even know what they are really seeking is salvation. Healing, wholeness. To have someone help them put back together the fragments of their lives. Only later will they be able to look back and realize how much a friend's look or touch, their words or their silent presence actually saved them.

Before King David was called out by Nathan the prophet, he didn't know he was in need of salvation either. But a friend speaking an honest word, a friend who dared to reach into the soul of a king and tell him he had been acting less than who he was created to be, brought him to his senses. Nathan brought salvation to his king and his friend.

Our Lenten journey this year invites us to reflect on the ways God brings salvation to us, too.

Most of the time we're not able to see that we are in need of being saved. We thought we took care of that when, at some point, we asked Jesus into our heart. But the truth is that salvation is more than a one-time thing. Like those young people at the shop or David staring into the eyes of his truth-telling friend or preachers who drive to coffee shops all flustered and out of sorts, it is only when we come into the presence of grace that we see just how much we still need to be saved. Over and over again.

I ended my shift at the coffee shop with Mark, another colleague. We speak about concerns of the day – car repairs and changed schedules. We talk about Lenten themes we plan to chase during this season, and about the practices of fasting that we'll each practice. Then I mark Mark on his forehead. *"Remember you are dust, and to dust you shall return."*

But then I add that we are sacred dust. So we trace in ash the image of the cross as the reminder that ash leads back to fire, and in the fire of divine love, God will one day make all things new. God will keep finding ways to save us in this life and the next.

So, at the end of this day, when you and I stare in the mirror tonight and will start to wash our faces, look closely one more time at the ashen cross. And remember it is the cross that lifts us out of the dust. It is the cross that, as Paul says, seems so foolish, but to we who are being saved, it is the power of God.

This is the Ash Wednesday Gospel as experienced at *Noble and Main*. Thanks be to God, who is saving us even now. Amen.

———

This Ash Wednesday reflection was written from notes made at Noble and Main Coffee Shop on February 26, 2020.

"More or Less?"

Have mercy on me, O God, because of your unfailing love. Because of your great compassion, blot out the stain of my sins. 2Wash me clean from my guilt. Purify me from my sin. 3For I recognize my shameful deeds — they haunt me day and night.

10Create in me a clean heart, O God. Renew a right spirit within me. 11Do not banish me from your presence, and don't take your Holy Spirit from me. 12Restore to me again the joy of your salvation, and make me willing to obey you. 13Then I will teach your ways to sinners, and they will return to you.

Psalms 51:1-19, *New Living Translations*

"Beware of practicing your piety before others in order to be seen by them; for then you have no reward from your Father in heaven. 2So whenever you give alms, do not sound a trumpet before you, as the hypocrites do in the synagogues and in the streets, so that they may be praised by others. Truly I tell you, they have received their reward. 3But when you give alms, do not let your left hand know what your right hand is doing, 4so that your alms may be done in secret; and your Father who sees in secret will reward you.

5 "And whenever you pray, do not be like the hypocrites; for they love to stand and pray in the synagogues and at the street corners, so that they may be seen by others. Truly I tell you, they have received their reward. 6But whenever you pray, go into your room and shut the door and pray to your Father who is in secret; and your Father who sees in secret will reward you.

7 "When you are praying, do not heap up empty phrases as the Gentiles do; for they think that they will be heard because of their many words. 8Do not be like them, for your Father knows what you need before you ask him.

9 Pray then in this way: Our Father in heaven, hallowed be your name. 10Your kingdom come. Your will be done, on earth as it is in heaven. 11Give us this day our daily bread.
12And forgive us our debts, as we also have forgiven our debtors.
13And do not bring us to the time of trial, but rescue us from the evil one. For the kingdom and the power and the glory are yours forever. Amen.

14 "For if you forgive others their trespasses, your heavenly Father will also forgive you; 15but if you do not forgive others, neither will your Father forgive your trespasses.

16 "And whenever you fast, do not look dismal, like the hypocrites, for they disfigure their faces so as to show others that they are fasting. Truly I tell you, they have received their reward. 17But when you fast, put oil on your head and wash your face, 18so that your fasting may be seen not by others but by your Father who is in secret; and your Father who sees in secret will reward you."

Matthew 6:1-18, *New Revised Standard Version*

"With a God like this loving you, you can pray very simply. Like this: 'Our Father in heaven, reveal who you are. 10Set the world right;
Do what's best — as above, so below.

11Keep us alive with three square meals. 12Keep us forgiven with you and forgiving others.
13Keep us safe from ourselves and the Devil.

Matthew 6:9-13, *The Message*

—————

A year ago, I was sitting in a coffee shop in town with one of my colleagues. I was beginning my "shift" for Ash Wednesday and our ecumenical *"Ashes to Go"* ministry that our local clergy group had shared for six or more years. My colleague marked me with ashes and then, turning to leave, offered what seemed to be unthinkable at the time:

"Have you thought about what it might be like to preach to an empty church on Easter?"

Most of us had barely even heard of Covid-19 a year ago. What we knew of it still seemed quite far away, remote from us in Cartersville. Quarantining for Easter? No way!

Three weeks later, schools shut down along with most everything that made up daily life for all of us at that time. And at Easter the sanctuary was empty and I had to hope someone was watching online so they could hear the "good news" of resurrection.

Now here it is a year later and because of Covid, I'm recording an Ash Wednesday reflection for our online-only Ash Wednesday worship service. We're still keeping distant from one another. No close-up face-to-face meetings, and certainly no touching, like marking one right after another with ashes on your forehead.

We have learned all too well this past year how fragile our world is, how much of our life can change in a New York minute. Covid still runs rampant in our world, infecting millions and claiming the lives of nearly half a million loved ones in the US alone. Which gives the words of this sacred day new meaning: *"Remember you are dust, and to dust you shall return."*

Those words are really an echo of the Prophet Joel's cry:

"Sound the alarm in Jerusalem! ... Blow the ram's horn in Jerusalem! Announce a time of fasting; call the people together for a solemn meeting. Gather all the people — the elders, the children, and even the babies" (Joel 2).

The crisis facing Israel then is no different than the crisis we've faced this past year — and still face. So on this Ash Wednesday, we sound the alarm, we blow the trumpet to get our attention and call us to new ways of thinking and living.

Like the people of Joel's day, we're asked to hit the pause button and re-examine our lives and our way of life. We're called to fasting, which seems difficult after a year in which most of us feel we have been on a 12-month fast from so much of life. None of us wants to give up anything else!

But what if we saw Lent as an invitation to experience more by doing less? Much of life was taken from us this past year. We had no choice but to give up much of our lives. But Lent invites us fast by *choosing* to give up some things and then offering them to God as a gift. By giving them to God, we create more space for us to experience God and others more deeply in our lives.

For with the God of abundant life, we discover that sometimes less really is more!

So we begin this holy season with ashes. We ask that the fire of God's love consume all that keeps us distant from God, distant from one another. And that, from the ashes, God would make all things new. That from the ashes new growth might emerge in us — new attitudes, new perspectives, new opportunities, new life. That less would become more.

We trace the cross in ash, not so that we can easily wash it away, but so we will understand that all ash comes from fire — specifically, this ash from the fire of divine love that is, even now, making all things new.

Wear the ash for a while. If you're seeing this at the middle of the day, mark yourself and let it be a sign to others as well as yourself. If you're seeing this at the end of the day, then before going to bed stare in the mirror and look closely one more time at the ashen cross. And remember it is the cross that lifts us out of the dust. It is the cross that, as Paul says, seems so foolish, but to we who are being saved, it is the power of God. It is the cross that, even now, is reconciling us to God, to one another and even to ourselves.

It is the cross that turns "less" into "more" — more grace than our guilt, more hope than our despair, even more life than death.

Let us, together, walk the road before us, and discover how much more God has to give us than we ever imagined possible. May it be so. Amen.

____

This Ash Wednesday reflection was shared online during the Covid pandemic on February 17, 2021.

"A Flock of Phoenixes"

*Jesus, full of the Holy Spirit, returned from the Jordan and
was led by the Spirit in the wilderness, 2where for forty
days he was tempted by the devil. He ate nothing at all
during those days, and when they were over, he was famished.*

*3The devil said to him, "If you are the Son of God,
command this stone to become a loaf of bread." 4Jesus
answered him, "It is written, 'One does not live by bread alone.'"*

*5Then the devil led him up and showed him in an instant
all the kingdoms of the world. 6And the devil said to him,
"To you I will give their glory and all this authority; for it has
been given over to me, and I give it to anyone I please.
7If you, then, will worship me, it will all be yours." 8Jesus
answered him, "It is written, 'Worship the Lord your God,
and serve only him.'"*

*9Then the devil took him to Jerusalem, and placed him on
the pinnacle of the temple, saying to him, "If you are the
Son of God, throw yourself down from here, 10for it is
written, 'He will command his angels concerning you, to
protect you,' 11and 'On their hands they will bear you up,
so that you will not dash your foot against a stone.'" 12Jesus
answered him, "It is said, 'Do not put the Lord
your God to the test.'"*

*13When the devil had finished every test, he departed from
him until an opportune time.*

Luke 4:1-13, *New Revised Standard Version*

If Lent happens to be new to you, a word of explanation might help at the outset. Lent is the season of 40 days plus 6 Sundays leading up to Easter. The word itself comes from an old English word that means "lengthen." It came to be associated with Spring, when the days "lengthen" (at least in the northern hemisphere!).

As with Spring, Lent is a time of growth, a time when new life emerges. For Christians, it's a time for reflection, repentance and renewal as we prepare to receive the wonder of the resurrection at Easter. Think of this season as Spring cleaning for the heart. During the next 40 days, we spend more time reading the Bible, praying, and reflecting on our relationship with Christ.

Throughout this season, we'll be using the idea of sharing the spiritual journey together. It's a reminder that, after a long couple of years of distancing, it's time to cozy up again! The reality is, we were created for community. We need each other. So what would it look like to renew our relationships and share a journey of faith together?

God promises that when we seek Him, we find Him. Perhaps we will discover that we find God in new ways when we look deeply into the faces of those created in the image of God. For today's reflection, I want to link this coming Sunday's Gospel lesson of Jesus in the wilderness with some thoughts about Ash Wednesday. So let's take a trip together and walk the road that lays ahead with Jesus and with one another.

———

As in past years, my reflection for this Ash Wednesday service flows (pun intended) from a coffee shop. For the past 8-9 years, the local clergy have taken "shifts" at a coffee shop and shared *"Ashes to Go"* – offering ashes to those who might not be able to attend a service, or who want to begin their day with the mark on their foreheads. In fact, I was re-reading part of a journal entry from the last time we did *Ashes to Go*. It was dated "February 26, 2020," meaning it was pre-pandemic. Three weeks later, the world shut down and a virus drove us away from one another. For months many of us did not worship in-person. We did very little of anything in-person. So to return to the coffee shop this year felt like something of a return to "normal."

And yet … Normal has left the building. In the past two years, three of my colleagues have left their places of ministry; one resigned and two others retired – including the person who usually organized our efforts. So today, I was the only one taking a shift at the coffee shop. But it has become one of my favorite ministry traditions.

In taking the ashes to a public place, each year I find new insights for the life of faith there in the coffee shop. And this year did not disappoint.

For our Lenten journey this year, I chose a theme about renewing our sense of community.

Social distancing pushed us away from one another. We lost the regular rhythm of being together at the same time in the same place. Not just here, but in churches all over. We've been slow to re-gather the scattered family of faith.

In some ways, the coffee shop reminds me of "church" when it's at its best. It's how people start their day – or in the case of church, their week. But people come to their favorite coffee shop not just to get a cup of Joe.

The people who work here know folks. *Noble and Main*, the hip coffee shop that used to be a gas station, has become a place of connection. It's not unlike the *Cheers* bar, "where everybody knows your name, and they're always glad you came."

I've not been a regular at the shop for a while. I've been more of a "special occasion" coffee shop attender lately – kind of like the Christmas and Easter crowd at churches! I had been gathering with a few colleagues on a weekly basis, but then came the holidays and surgery and recovery for the first few weeks of January. Throw in everyone else's hectic schedules and we've been thrown off our routine.

So when I arrive at the shop and ask the young woman at the counter about using a table for *Ashes to Go*, she hesitates. She has no idea who I am. "I'll ask." She steps toward the back of the preparation island to talk with Katie, one of the staffers. Thankfully when she sees me she recognizes me. "Of course," she says with a smile as she walks toward me. "You all do this each year," she adds. And the young woman's hesitation melts away. She then turns to me and takes my coffee order and smiles as she asks what I would like.

"Good morning," I say to her, and then add, "That's where I should have started." I realized that that had said good morning earlier but I had not really said it *to her*. It was just a phrase I used to get to get to my request; they were not words spoken to *connect* with her. So I start again. And fortunately, she cuts me a break and doesn't seem offended. Grace abounds!

I take a seat at a table in the back and set up. A bowl of ashes, a napkin for my fingers, and a cup of coffee. I snap a picture and post it to the church's *Facebook* page to let folks know I'll be here today. Only then do I survey the room.

Scattered around the shop are a handful of others. It strikes me that most, like me, have come alone. At the table in front of me a man works by himself on his laptop. He occasionally makes calls, his earbuds stuffed on each side of his head, but mostly he seems off in his own world. And yet, he is *here* – in a *public* place surrounded by others and by the noises of a coffee machine grinding coffee beans and by the crunch of ice being scooped out for an iced coffee to go. If it's quiet and solitude he wants, he won't find it here.

And then it occurs to me that while he may come here alone, it's not because he wants to be alone. Something in him – something in all of us – longs for others.

Another younger man also works on his laptop. His coffee companion from earlier left long ago. But he remains. Is it for the coffee? No; his cup is empty and hasn't been touched for quite some time. Is it the free Wi-Fi? Maybe. But again he chooses a *public* place to be alone.

Two couples sit to my left and right. To the left is a young man who came in with an older woman – someone who appears to be his grandmother, not his mother. He sat down while she ordered some food and coffee; now she makes her way to the table to join him. He has looked at his phone nonstop since coming in and he continues to do so. They have not said more than a couple words since sitting down a half hour earlier. They split a bagel and share in a silent, private communion. It's not that he's ignored her. It simply seems they are comfortable with each other and don't need words. When they leave, he takes the empty plate and their cups to the counter. And as they walk toward the door, I watch as he places his hand in the middle of her back as if to steady her. It's a tender gesture of care and affection.

To my right, another couple sits and doesn't say much either. He walks to the table while she orders their coffee. He grimaces with each step. "How are you doing?" I ask as he looks over at me and gives me a quick up/down glance. He seems to be trying to figure out what the guy with a bow tie, a stole around his shoulders and a black cross on his forehead is doing. "Oh I'm hanging in there," he replies. He grimaces as he sits down.

"Hanging by a thread or by your fingernails?" I ask him. He describes a recent back injury and now the pain etched on his face makes sense. His wife joins him with their coffee and they both bury their heads in their phones for the next 30 minutes. Only occasionally do they share a few words. Yet it's clear they want to be here *together*.

Others come and go before the familiar face of my friend and colleague, Mark, shows up at the table. We spend the next half hour talking fast and furious. He asks about my surgery; I ask about his recent call to go serve at a church in another state — a call he just made public this past weekend to the church he has served for 24 years. We linger together, knowing that these kinds of conversations will not be possible much longer. I mark him with ashes before he goes and feel the tug of already saying goodbye.

Soon a small group of three comes in. They look to be a church staff team having a meeting.

One of them calls a server by name and waves. After their coffee comes, they dive into a planning session with intensity.

Then a young woman comes in. She carries her coffee in one hand and with the other, holds a phone pressed to her ear and talks in hushed tones. As she talks quietly, I return to jotting down my thoughts. And then I hear a sniffle. I look up as she brushes a tear away from each of her eyes. She thanks whoever is on the call with her and lays her phone down. More tears.

Over and over I see the scene repeat as individuals wander in as if wandering in some kind of wilderness. They come alone and yet come to this familiar place where they are not alone. Even those who come with others and sit in silence come here together. Because somehow, in this place they are sipping from the cup of comfort and connection. Here they find reassurance that will flavor the rest of their day.

I listen to the muffled tones of voices mingling with the music. I listen as the staff offer greetings to customers. And as I listen, I realize they are saying more than what type of coffee they want or whether they want room for cream. Hidden in the small talk is the unspoken need: *Do you see me? Can you hear me?*

To be seen; to be heard; to be valued. It is what brings them here – and what brings me here too.

It's a reminder that we really are created for community. Isolation doesn't serve any of us well. We need each other. We reach for each other just by being in a place with others, or by hearing a familiar voice on a phone call or by sitting at the table. We need each other as we make plans to do something meaningful, or as we offer the quick touch of a fist bump when running into someone we know, or in the firm embrace of a friend like Mark as we hug goodbye.

We need each other to confess as I overhear one of the trio describe something that didn't work out like expected. He adds that it wasn't his fault but speaks it as if he doesn't believe what he just said. We need each other to share ideas and help us dream about what could be even after things have gone awry. We need each other to pour a cup of coffee and hand it to us with a smile like Caroline does for me. We need each other for support, for care, for help to steady us on our feet. We need each other for assurance that we are not alone. We need each other to tell us that we matter. We need each other to be in a place where we are surrounded by the noises and voices of life to remind us that we too are alive.

When I get up to go for a refill on my coffee the young woman whose tears continue to trickle down her face looks up. "Are you OK?" I ask quietly. Her eyes well up. "Yes," she replies, and then contradicts her own answer by telling me she is "just" going through some difficulties right now. She thanks me for asking. "That's sweet of you," she says, looking at me as if I am her grandfather. She musters a smile even as she wipes away another tear.

In the middle of writing these thoughts my pen runs dry. My first thought is to go out to my car where I have another pen. But instead I go to the counter and ask one of the guys, Aaron and Parker: "Do you have a pen?" Aaron smiles and reaches into a cup full of pens. "Sure," he says and hands me a neon-green pen.

It's something simple but it is also a reminder that I also have a need – that I, too, also have a need of others. Yet it also reminds me of something more important. I could have handled that need "on my own," I think to myself. But then I think better. *Why? Why would I do that when I can reach out? When I could connect?"*

As I take the pen, Aaron and Parker both smile. My need fulfills a need they have – a need we all have. We all have a need to be needed. A pen is no big deal and yet it is. To ask and to receive. To be asked and to give. It's what we all want and it's what we all need.

As I'm jotting notes, I see out the corner of my eye the young woman packing up to go. She walks over to the table and thanks me again for asking about her. To my surprise, she shares even more. She has just gone through a break-up. Her face reflects the pain of it. And then her sister – the voice on the other end of the phone earlier – had just gotten engaged. One person's dream come true adds salt to her wound.

But then she adds, "I'm a believer," and she starts to speak about how God's grace comes at unexpected times. "You did that with your concern," she says and thanks me again as she turns to go.

To ask. To give. Perhaps it is the simple things we do that help us hear the voice of God when we most need it.

The restroom in the coffee shop is occupied so I walk next door to the meeting room used by the shop owners for overflow crowds. A handful of individuals are there – all at separate tables. Yet again, it strikes me that they choose to come to a *public* place to be alone. As I walk back through the room, a young man named Vadeem stops me. He notices the stole around my neck. "Is it from Ukraine?" he asks. "Mexico," I tell him. He says the design reminds him of handiwork from Ukraine. He then begins to tell me he has family in Ukraine. I tell him he must be very concerned for them, and he says that his family lives in the western part of the country, near Lviv, not far from the border of Poland. So far, no Russian fighting has broken out there.

But then he adds that his wife's family is in Kyiv, hunkered down in a basement. I pull up a chair and listen as he describes their daily calls and updates. They describe the bombs they hear, the uncertainty they feel. His deep concern for them is written on his face. He then speaks of a pastor there who had a vision two weeks ago to stock up on supplies – things like gas and food. Do it "for the flock," the vision had told him. Now the man is caring for his church community with those supplies. I thank him for sharing and we shake hands. That he chose to tell me – *a stranger* – amazes me.

I return to my table in the main part of the shop. An elderly man named Ron, age 78 (I know because one of the first things he told me was his age), approaches the table. He's been in the shop for a couple of hours. Now he makes his way to my table. He is stooped over, unable to stand straight. Old age is taking its toll, he tells me. He also tells me he usually meets with his pastor, but he couldn't come today. And then he pours out 78 years of his life story in five minutes. Baptized at age seven but done only to please his mother. Time in the military (he still wears dog tags). He became an advertising executive who had successfully climbed the corporate ladder. Young and carefree he had no thought of ever getting married. And then he met the love of his life. They've now been married 41 years.

Then his face turns serious. In his old age he had realized that despite his success and wealth, "I wasn't happy." A little more than two months ago he had a religious experience and had been baptized. Aging was making him re-think his life. "Death is the great equalizer," he quietly admits. We shake hands and he goes back to his table by the window. As he walks away, I wonder what makes a person share such intimate details with a total stranger.

Because he *needed* to tell me his story. Even though his pastor was not available to meet, he had come here to the shop. He was still looking to connect and to belong; still longing to be seen and heard.

It is our story, each of us. It is Jesus' story, too. He wanders into the wilderness and finds Himself in a strange place facing great challenges. He seems to come there alone. And yet He is not. Each time He quotes scripture, He is drawing on the voices of His ancestors. He listens to their wisdom and finds courage to face whatever is being thrown at Him.

And so we go to coffee shops or to church because it is in those places that we learn to ask for help or learn to give something back. We come with our frailties and our successes; our hurts and our hopes. Like ashes on our foreheads, we can see the same marks on everyone around us. The marks we wear help us to know at least that we are not alone in the wilderness we each face. To know that there are voices in us and around us, reminding us that we all belong to each other. We go in hopes of seeing God around us and discovering God within us. We were created to share such moments.

And while the Lenten season invites us to remember we are dust and to dust we shall return, it also reminds us that there is something beautiful in us that can be shared. We may be dust, but we are sacred dust.

This is the hope we all have – to love and to be loved; to share ourselves with another; to find a connection that makes us feel like we are more than dust; to hear a word that allows us to become more than dust.

The wilderness tries to tell us otherwise. Tries to isolate us, make us doubt, cause us to give up on our faith, on others, and ourselves. Like Jesus, we must close our eyes and listen for the voices of those around us, friends and strangers. It is the community that amplifies the whisper of God's voice, *"You are my beloved; and with you I am well pleased"* so that we can hear it even way out in the wilderness.

And then, like a flock of wild phoenixes, we will rise from the ashes of our lives to new life. This is the Ash Wednesday/Lenten Gospel from the hip coffee shop on Main Street. Thanks be to God. Amen.

———

This reflection was compiled from journal notes made on Ash Wednesday, March 2, 2022, and adapted for a community Lenten Lunch reflection shared on Thursday, March 3, 2022.

"Common Grounds"

But whenever you pray, go into your room and shut the door and pray to your Father who is in secret; and your Father who sees in secret will reward you. … 9 Pray then in this way:

Our Father in heaven, hallowed be your name. 10Your kingdom come. Your will be done, on earth as it is in heaven.

11Give us this day our daily bread. 12And forgive us our debts, as we also have forgiven our debtors. 13And do not bring us to the time of trial, but rescue us from the evil one.

For the kingdom and the power and the glory are yours forever. Amen."

Matthew 6:6, 9-13, *New Revised Standard Version*

The Ash Wednesday reflection was brewed fresh this afternoon from time spent at *Noble and Main* coffee shop earlier today. Serving *"Ashes to Go"* at a coffee shop has been one of the highlights of ministry throughout my time in Cartersville. Other than two years ago when a pandemic outbreak prevented it, *Ashes to Go* has been an annual part of my Lenten journey for the past decade. Taking a church rite outside the walls of the church to people who might not be able to attend a service or who hadn't considered going has proven deeply meaningful.

The shop attracts people of all ages and life experiences. As I observe those who come in, it becomes clear that they come there seeking more than coffee. There are other places to get coffee. But they come here. They feel connected to the people here. Even if they come alone they know they are not alone. Not everyone stays. Some come for take-out and leave with more than one cup, a sign that they will be meeting someone somewhere. It reminds me that the Lenten journey, like a good cup of coffee, is best shared.

For our Lenten journey this year, I chose the theme about traveling with good company. We all know how good companions enrich a road trip. We see and experience more than if left on our own. During our Lenten journey this year, the scripture stories will bring us alongside a host of companions to share the journey. The names will be familiar. Adam and Eve, Abraham and Sarah, Moses, Ezekiel, King David; Nicodemus, an unnamed Samaritan woman, a man born blind, two sisters and a brother plunged into grief, the Apostle Paul, Jesus. We'll need a bus to fit them all in. Just because they are mentioned in the Bible we think they are so different. But the truth is these salty saints are much like us and they have much to teach us.

And so do the people at the coffee shop. Beginning with the coffee shop owner Madi who stops by a table where I have been talking with friends and offers a gracious welcome. She had already responded to my e-mail asking permission to share the ashes. She gladly invited me to do so again. Benton takes my order at the counter. He is a high school student who is working this morning only because his school is on winter break. A senior, he hopes to go to UGA next year and major in marketing. He takes my order and then when I refill my cup later doesn't charge me full price.

Cassidy is the newest face for me among those working at the shop. She works on my order while I am talking and then rather than shout out a name, she walks out from behind the counter and delivers my cup to me. A kind and thoughtful gesture.

Even before I can sit, I see Matt and his wife and their four-year-old daughter Abigail. They have all come here for a cup of coffee before school. Matt tells me he has just returned from South Africa and that until he saw the cross on my forehead, he didn't know what day it was.

When I ask what was happening in South Africa, he shares that his own ministry has taken him in a new direction this past year. He left the church he served last August, something that I had not heard. He is now working with an organization that identifies indigenous leaders and helps them connect to resources that will enable them to do their work better. He sounds excited about it.

It seems that the theme of transitions will run throughout the day. No sooner do I get settled in at a table than a former church member (Samantha) comes in. As I speak to her, her eyes brim with tears even as she is smiling. She tells me that the previous night she had been thinking about needing to give me a call this week. When she woke up and saw the *Facebook* post, she took it as a message from God and determined to come by before going to work across the street. She alludes to changes but quickly says she is not quite ready to talk about them. And yet the longer she sits there the more she begins to share. A new job, changes in family life, preparing for a new home and moving next month. Lots going on.

As I dip my finger into the bowl of ashes, I ask her

what the ashes will mean for her this year. She thinks for a moment and then replies, "That you can't do this alone." She describes how the cross has a bar across it and says, "You need others." She then begins to describe the support she's already received and how she's being carried in some way. She has not been alone. She sounds healthy and most of all hopeful. I mark her with the ashes and tell her it is the sign of God's presence with her and of the companions who join her. And though the wilderness may be difficult, there is always new life beyond it. "And you will not be alone."

No sooner does she leave than Doug comes in. I see him looking around the shop and then he spies me at the table. He walks over and says he had come today wondering if anyone would be sharing ashes. He gives me a big bear hug and we immediately start talking about our memories of sharing ashes together in previous years. It was comical that one year, he and I covered about a third of day – two Baptists leading this very non-Baptist tradition! He speaks of changes too. He's still fresh in the job at the Good Neighbor Shelter and navigating the challenges. He is experiencing some personal renewal, painful because it has meant shedding some things that have been hindering him. He describes it as a fire.

I remind him that where there is fire, there will be ashes. "What then will these ashes mean for you this year?" He replies, "A sign of God's presence and God's leadership," he replies. As I mark him, I remind him of words I have shared with him before: "We are dust and to dust we shall return." But, I add, God says, "We are sacred dust." I use the former church member's image of the cross – one way connecting him to God, and the crossbar connecting him to others. "You are not alone for the adventure ahead." And I assure him that God goes with him too – above and behind, beneath and beside and within him. We embrace again with a promise to share breakfast in the next couple of weeks.

As Doug leaves, Chris, a former *Leadership Bartow* friend, has come in to pick up coffee.

We stand and talk for a few minutes. He too is in transition. He has been named as the new director for the Bartow Collaborative, Doug's previous role. It strikes me that he looks like a smaller version of Doug – stocky frame and beard, but with hair on his head!

In just this first hour the morning has been full of meaningful moments. It will be a memorable day if that's all that happens. I am grateful that in the 12 years here in Cartersville I've been enriched with these friendships. I am more blessed than I have realized.

With a lull in people seeking the ashes, I finally have time to look around at who else is here today. There is a woman who came in about the same time as me this morning who has been diligently working on her computer at the next table. Behind her a man in a flannel shirt and a black ball cap has been staring intently at his laptop screen, occasionally sipping on an iced coffee. He wears earbuds that hang down from his head; I notice a slight rhythmic movement of his shoulders and it tells me he is keeping time with the beat of music.

As I step to the counter to order another coffee I watch as a man and woman carry on a silent conversation. It is their hands that speak. She looks on in deep concern as his hands tell her a story. He stops as Cassidy brings their drinks to them. He looks up and then touches his hand to his mouth and gestures outwardly toward her. I know this sign: *"Thank you."* Gracious words returned for an act of kindness.

Two women carry on an intense conversation behind my right shoulder. Over my left shoulder I hear a man's voice talking on the phone with someone. Sitting to my right is a man who sips his coffee and munches on a pastry while scrolling through his phone on the table. The sound of a fan fills the air. Then a spurt of customers comes in and the folks behind the counter whirl into action.

My stomach growls. Loudly. Black coffee is not enough to quiet it. On any other day I could skip breakfast and my stomach would not care. But because I am fasting today it decides to make a fuss.

All three workers are talking with customers but it is clear it's about more than their order.

One of the guests recognizes the man sitting to my right. She approaches his table and they begin to catch up. "I retired," I hear her say, adding that it had been prompted by a recent surgery.

More transitions. He tells her about some new work he is doing and later I overhear the words "studio" and "artist."

A mom with three young children comes in – twin girls who look to be around three and a boy with tousled blonde hair and a backpack who stands a head taller than his sisters. The two girls sport matching pink backpacks with "My Pony" faces on the back. She uses a card to pay and then lets each of the three touch the screen to finish payment. Three steps, three fingers to verify them.

As she talks to them she bends or stoops to look them in the face. Not once does she speak to them without getting down to their level. She opens the door for them and they follow with a drink and a muffin on shiny aluminum trays balanced carefully in their small hands.

Tamara stands at the counter and then walks over and sits down. She is curious. When I ask her if she would like to have the ashes she gives a cheerful yes. She grew up a Methodist, she tells me, so it's a familiar tradition. Now she attends another church in town. She welcomes the words about being dust but also being sacred dust. I remind her that God goes with us in whatever wilderness we face with a promise there is a resurrection on the other side. "Amen!" she says enthusiastically and as she leaves she wishes me "a blessed day."

The pace of customers picks up. Five people wait as the sound of grinders and frothers fill the air. A young mother carries a baby in a car seat. Two women who look to be sisters come in. A nurse leaves with a coffee. All kinds of people coming and going. The place is filled with more energy than I usually see when I visit.

Leigh Jones from First Presbyterian arrives to take a shift. We are playing tag team ashes today.

We talk about church life and the post-pandemic challenges but also the opportunities. Much of her time in town has been lived under the shadow of the pandemic. To emerge from the cloud is a relief, and yet so much has changed that creates challenges for church life – all of life really. We're all still figuring our way forward, making a road by walking it. The cross of ashes is our guide, a reminder to walk in the way of love. The ashes are a symbol of hope that the fires we may have experienced have refined us for whatever lies ahead. The ash is what we leave behind as we rise to new life.

Throughout the day I have prefaced the imposition of ashes with a question: *"What do the ashes mean for you today?"* The responses have been unique and revealing. For Leigh, it is a sign of her dependence on God and a challenge to deepen faith during the Lenten journey ahead. I remind her of God's presence with her for that journey and that she goes under the sign of the cross. We then trade chairs and then I give her my stole to wear while she begins her shift.

I come back a little over an hour and a half later and she tells me about the people who've stopped by the table, some seeking the ashes and some just curious as to what she is doing. It takes us back to our earlier conversation about how the church must take its message on the road out among where people work and play and live most of their lives.

After Lee leaves a woman named Marcita comes into the coffee shop. She looks around and then spies me and points in my direction as she walks toward me. A friend had told her that there would be ashes available here at the shop. She stopped because she is unable to attend services at her own Lutheran church this evening. *"What will the ashes will mean for you this season?"* Without pausing to think, she speaks about wanting to share her faith today. She hopes the ashes on her forehead will be a message to others about God's love and that they might come to know that love. I mark her with the cross, which serves as a commissioning for bearing witness to God's love in her life.

Leigh Anne comes in and quickly works her way to the table. She is full of energy and smiling. She has taken her lunch break from teaching 7th graders in order to receive the ashes for the rest of the day. She tells me she knows she cannot tell students about her faith, but she can answer their questions when they ask her about it. We talk about her care for aging parents who live several states away. She has been driving back and forth nearly every weekend to see them. She describes it as a season of life that she is in and that though it is difficult it is a meaningful season to spend this time with her parents.

"What will the ashes mean for you?" I ask. Her eyes began to well up. "God's love," she says, marveling that God would send His only Son to die so that we might live. She speaks of how faith is so central to her life now she cannot imagine living life without God's presence. I mark her with the cross, using her words of the sign of God's love for her and presence with her.

The spouse of a clergy colleague waits beside the table for us to finish talking. No sooner does Leigh Anne get up than he immediately takes her seat. A schedule conflict will prevent him from attending services at his own church so he came here. When I ask him what it means for him, he also speaks of changes and needing strength. A deeper trust, a more consistent practice, God's peace. As I trace the ashen cross on his forehead, I remind him he is not alone. We hug and then he leaves.

No sooner does he walk away than Pat McCoy comes in. We talk about health issues and family concerns.

What do the ashes mean for her? "Gratitude," she replies. She finishes physical therapy this week following shoulder surgery several months ago. Gratitude that her sister has come through brain surgery. Gratitude for family members and friends in her life. Gratitude for parents who first passed on the richness of faith to her. She leaves, but not without expressing her gratitude to me.

Throughout the day I have listened to the machines in the background as they grind coffee.

Those grounds become the basis for all kinds of drinks – hot ones and cold ones, ones with cream and sugar, some without; cappuccinos and macchiatos and espressos. And yet they all share one thing in common: the grounds. Common coffee grounds.

And like the coffee I have been drinking at the shop, each of us brings our own flavors to the cups that hold our lives. There is so much that appears to be different about us all, but I realize those are just the additives, the creams and sugars and ice and fancy foam that rests on top.

But at the heart of things we all share common grounds. We have the common need to connect with someone else and to be heard. We all have our own set of hopes. Each of us carries heavy burdens and the weight of them sometimes becomes great enough that our eyes well up with tears.

It is our story, each of us. Whether we have ashes on our forehead or not, we know that life is brief. We've each been scorched beyond what we ever thought we could stand and aspects of our lives are left behind in ashes. Yet somehow, we made it through the wilderness because we were never alone there.

We need each other. We were created to share such moments. So we look for places where we can do just that. And as I saw today, our local coffee shop offers a safe place to share our lives. At our local shop, we can at least be in the presence of a person who will give us something warm to hold when life feels cold.

In those simple lovely moments, we are reminded that while we may be dust, we are sacred dust. When we share that common ground, we hear God's voice most clearly. We are reminded we are not alone. And that by walking together, we don't get lost in the wilderness. Rather we help each other go through it and find new life on the other side.

This is the Ash Wednesday Gospel from the shop at the corner of Noble and Main. May we drink deeply from the cup of hope that God is with us. And may that awareness lead us to repent and believe – and live – this Good News together. Thanks be to God. Amen.

———

This reflection was compiled from journal notes made on Ash Wednesday, February 22, 2023.